Recipe Collection

APPETIZERS

Publications International Ltd.

Favorite Brand Name Recipes at www.fbnr.com

Louis Weber, CEO
Publications International, Ltd.
7373 North Cicero Avenue
Lincolnwood, IL 60712

Recipes developed and tested by Land O'Lakes Test Kitchens. For questions regarding recipes in this cookbook or LAND O LAKES® products, call 1-800-328-4155.

Special thanks to the staff of Land O'Lakes, Inc., including Amy Jeatran, Publisher; Becky Wahlund, Director of Test Kitchens; Marge Ryerson, Editor; and Pat Weed, Publications Coordinator.

Pictured on the front cover: Cheesy Roasted Red Pepper Crostini (page 70).

Pictured on the back cover: Mushroom Pinwheels (page 75), Onion & Garlic Crostini (page 30), Warm Spinach Dip (page 58).

ISBN-13: 978-1-4127-2672-6
ISBN-10: 1-4127-2672-7

Manufactured in China.

8 7 6 5 4 3 2 1

Preparation and Cooking Times: All recipes were developed and tested in the Land O'Lakes Test Kitchens by professional home economists. Use "Preparation Time" and "Cooking, Baking, Microwaving or Broiling Time" given with each recipe as guides. Preparation time is based on the approximate amount of "active" time required to assemble the recipe. This includes steps such as chopping, mixing, cooking pasta, frosting, etc. Cooking, baking, microwaving or broiling times are based on the minimum amount of time required for these recipe steps.

CONTENTS

22

52

66

92

APPETIZERS

It's better with butter

How can I make my appetizer table look more attractive? Liven up basic stoneware with boldly colored or patterned serving platters or bowls, and accent the table with bright napkins. Fresh or dried flowers reflecting the colors of the season will brighten a sideboard, mantle, or dining room table, as will simple votive candles. Festive garlands and ribbons, holiday ornaments, fresh evergreen branches, and pine cones placed on the table around the serving plates and platters also add panache.

How many different kinds of appetizers should be served at a party? No matter how large the party, two or three kinds of pre-dinner appetizers are sufficient—a combination of hot and cold appetizers, a dip or spread, and a meatless option makes for a nice assortment.

Count five to six "bites" per person during the standard cocktail hour. If the appetizers are replacing dinner, plan 10 to 12 "bites" per guest and offer five or six different choices. If you're still concerned about having enough, make 10 to 20 percent extra of the items that can be frozen if not used.

How can I keep hot appetizers hot and cold appetizers cold? Electric warming trays, slow cookers, chafing dishes, and fondue pots are invaluable for use at the serving table. If you don't have any of these, serve hot foods in casserole dishes that hold heat for a relatively long time. Keep cold appetizers cold by storing them in the refrigerator until serving time, then place the containers or plates in a bowl with crushed ice or over an ice pack.

10

28

51

Cheese Know-How

Buying & Serving Cheese

- If you're serving only cheese, fruit, bread, and crackers at a party, allow 3 to 4 ounces of cheese per person. If other foods will be offered, 2 ounces per person should be adequate.

- For a large group, you might want to include up to six different cheeses on your cheese tray. For smaller groups, three types are sufficient.

- A good mix of cheeses includes a hard or semihard cheese like Cheddar; a mild, semisoft variety like Havarti; and a soft ripened cheese such as Brie or Camembert. See "Types of Cheese" for additional options.

- Label cheeses so guests can identify what they are sampling.

Types of Cheese

- Hard or semihard: Asiago, Cheddar, Colby, Edam, Gouda, Parmesan, Provolone, Swiss.

- Semisoft: American, Blue Cheese, Brick, Colby, Gorgonzola, Havarti, Monterey Jack, Mozzarella, Muenster, Roquefort.

- Soft: Brie, Camembert, Feta, Chèvre (goat cheese).

Cheese Cutting Tips

- Cheese is easiest to cut when it's cold.

- Use a clean, sharp knife to cut cheese.

- Cut cheese wheels into wedges. Cut rectangular, square, and cylindrical cheese into slices. Cut wedges or triangular cheese into thin wedges. Cheese can also be cut into cubes.

- Use a serrated cutter to make attractive crinkle-cut shapes.

- If you're preparing a snack tray, try cutting a variety of shapes using a knife or small canapé or cookie cutter.

46

62

83

GAME DAY PARTY

Tired of takeout pizza as party food? Kick off your next game day celebration with these recipes. They're the perfect picks to keep the whole gang well-fed and focused on the game. No matter how your team does, everyone is a winner with these great snacks and appetizers.

BLT Focaccia Squares

Preparation time: **40 minutes** | Baking time: **22 minutes** | **32 appetizers**

  1 (1-pound) loaf frozen white bread dough, thawed
  2 tablespoons mayonnaise
  2 teaspoons Dijon-style mustard
  ¼ teaspoon freshly ground black pepper
  4 to 5 (1½ cups) Roma tomatoes, chopped
  ½ pound (about 8 slices) crisply cooked bacon, crumbled
  6 ounces (1½ cups) LAND O LAKES® Monterey Jack Cheese, shredded
  ⅓ cup sliced green onions
  1 cup thinly sliced romaine lettuce leaves

• Heat oven to 400°F. Stretch or roll bread dough into greased 15×10×1-inch jelly-roll pan. (If dough is difficult to stretch, cover with plastic food wrap and let rest 10 minutes, then continue stretching to fit into pan.)

• Combine mayonnaise, mustard and pepper in small bowl. Spread evenly over dough. Combine tomatoes, bacon, ¾ cup cheese and green onions in medium bowl; toss lightly. Sprinkle over dough.

• Bake for 20 to 25 minutes or until edges of crust are golden brown. Sprinkle with remaining cheese; continue baking just until cheese is melted (2 to 3 minutes). Immediately sprinkle with lettuce. Cut into squares. Serve warm.

Cajun Potato Wedges

Preparation time: **15 minutes** | Baking time: **25 minutes** | **10 servings**

Potatoes

¼ cup LAND O LAKES® Butter

1 tablespoon Cajun seasoning

2 (16-ounce) packages frozen potato wedges, thawed

Sauce

1½ cups LAND O LAKES® Sour Cream

4 ounces (1 cup) LAND O LAKES® Cheddar Cheese, shredded

¼ cup chopped green onions

¼ cup milk

¼ teaspoon garlic salt

4 to 6 drops hot pepper sauce

LAND O LAKES® Cheddar Cheese, shredded, if desired

• Heat oven to 425°F. Combine butter and Cajun seasoning in 1-quart saucepan; heat until sizzling. Spread out potatoes on two greased aluminum foil-lined baking sheets with sides. Drizzle evenly with butter mixture; toss to coat. Bake for 25 to 30 minutes or until potatoes are golden brown and crisp.

• Meanwhile, combine all sauce ingredients in medium bowl; mix until well blended. Spoon into serving bowl; garnish with additional shredded cheese, if desired. Serve potatoes with sauce.

tip:

The cheesy sour cream sauce could also be used on hot baked potatoes.

Zesty Sour Cream Dips

Preparation time: **10 minutes** | **8 servings**

Cilantro-Lime

- 1 cup LAND O LAKES® Sour Cream
- ¼ cup chopped fresh cilantro leaves
- ¼ cup sliced green onions
- 2 tablespoons fresh lime juice
- 1 teaspoon finely chopped fresh garlic
- ¼ teaspoon salt
- Freshly grated lime peel, if desired

• Combine all ingredients in small bowl; mix well. Cover; refrigerate until serving time.

Terrific Taco

- 1 cup LAND O LAKES® Sour Cream
- 1½ teaspoons dry taco seasoning mix

• Combine all ingredients in small bowl; mix well. Cover; refrigerate until serving time.

Hot & Fiery

- 1 cup LAND O LAKES® Sour Cream
- ¼ cup hot 'n spicy mayonnaise or salad dressing*
- 1 tablespoon chipotle chiles in adobe sauce, chopped

• Combine all ingredients in small bowl; mix well. Cover; refrigerate until serving time.

*Substitute ¼ cup salsa.

tip:
Canned chipotle peppers are very hot and spicy. A little goes a long way! Store leftovers in resealable plastic freezer bag and place in the freezer for future use.

Avocado & Chile Quesadillas

Preparation time: **25 minutes** | Baking time: **9 minutes** | **16 servings**

- 1 medium (¾ cup) ripe avocado, mashed
- 1 medium (½ cup) tomato, seeded, chopped
- 1 tablespoon seeded chopped jalapeño chiles
- 1 tablespoon chopped fresh cilantro
- ¼ teaspoon salt
- 3 tablespoons LAND O LAKES® Butter, melted
- 8 (8-inch) flour tortillas
- 6 ounces (1½ cups) LAND O LAKES® Hot Pepper Jack Cheese, shredded

    LAND O LAKES® Sour Cream
    Red or green salsa

• Heat oven to 500°F. Adjust rack to lowest position. Mash avocado in medium bowl with fork until almost smooth. Stir in tomato, chiles, cilantro and salt.

• Brush 1 side of each of 4 tortillas with half of melted butter. Place tortillas onto large ungreased baking sheet, buttered-side down. Spread about ¼ cup avocado mixture onto each tortilla; sprinkle each evenly with ¼ cup cheese. Top with remaining 4 tortillas. Brush top of tortillas with remaining melted butter.

• Place another large ungreased baking sheet on top of quesadillas to prevent puffing. Bake for 6 to 8 minutes or until bottoms are golden brown. Remove top baking sheet. Turn quesadillas; continue baking for 3 to 4 minutes or until bottoms are golden brown.

• To serve, cut each quesadilla into wedges with sharp knife, kitchen shears or pizza cutter. Serve hot with sour cream and salsa.

Indian-Spiced Chicken Wings

Preparation time: **10 minutes** | Baking time: **30 minutes** | **24 drumettes**

  4 teaspoons curry powder
  2 teaspoons ground ginger
  1 teaspoon ground cinnamon
  ¼ teaspoon salt
  2 pounds (24) chicken wing drumettes
  3 tablespoons LAND O LAKES® Butter, melted
  1 cup mango chutney

• Place curry powder, ginger, cinnamon and salt in large resealable plastic food storage bag. Add chicken; seal. Shake bag until chicken is evenly coated with spices. Refrigerate for at least 3 hours or overnight.

• Heat oven to 350°F. Arrange chicken on aluminum foil-lined 15×10×1-inch jelly-roll pan. Drizzle with butter. Bake for 30 to 35 minutes or until chicken is golden brown and crisp and juices run clear when pierced with a fork.

• Serve chicken with chutney.

tip:
Look for a variety of chutney flavors at the supermarket. Mango chutney is the most classic, but apple, peach and ginger chutneys would be equally delicious with the chicken.

Hot Pepper Vegetable Dip

Preparation time: **15 minutes** | 2½ cups

  1 cup LAND O LAKES® Sour Cream
  ¼ cup milk
  1 (8-ounce) package cream cheese, softened
  ¼ cup chopped ripe olives
  4 ounces (1 cup) LAND O LAKES® Hot Pepper Monterey Jack Cheese, shredded
  1 (2-ounce) jar diced pimientos, drained
  1 tablespoon sliced green onion
  ⅛ to ¼ teaspoon hot pepper sauce
     Fresh vegetables (red bell pepper strips, green bell pepper strips, pea pods, carrot sticks, etc.)

• Combine sour cream, milk and cream cheese in small bowl. Beat at medium speed, scraping bowl often, until smooth.

• Stir in all remaining ingredients except vegetables. Cover; refrigerate at least 2 hours. Serve with vegetables.

tip:
Omit ¼ cup milk for a thicker consistency.

Sweet & Sour Meatballs

Preparation time: **45 minutes** | Baking time: **40 minutes** | **5 dozen meatballs**

Meatballs

- ½ cup dried bread crumbs
- 1 pound lean ground beef
- 1 (12-ounce) package spicy bulk pork sausage
- 1 egg
- ½ teaspoon dry mustard
- 1 tablespoon soy sauce

Sauce

- 1 (20-ounce) can pineapple chunks in juice, drained, reserve juice
- 2 tablespoons firmly packed brown sugar
- 1 tablespoon cornstarch
- 2 tablespoons cider vinegar
- 1 tablespoon soy sauce
- ½ teaspoon ground ginger
- 2 medium green and/or red bell peppers, cut into 1-inch pieces

• Heat oven to 350°F. Stir together all meatball ingredients in large bowl. Shape meatball mixture into 1-inch balls. Place meatballs onto ungreased 15×10×1-inch jelly roll pan. Bake for 15 to 20 minutes or until meatballs are browned.

• Meanwhile, combine reserved pineapple juice, brown sugar, cornstarch, vinegar, 1 tablespoon soy sauce and ginger in 1-quart saucepan. Cook over medium heat, stirring occasionally, until mixture is thickened and bubbly (4 to 6 minutes). Boil, stirring constantly, 1 minute.

• Place meatballs, sauce, pineapple chunks and bell peppers in ungreased 2-quart casserole; stir gently to coat. Cover; bake for 25 to 30 minutes or until meatballs are heated through. Serve in chafing dish with toothpicks or keep warm in slow cooker.

Garlic Football Toast

Preparation time: **40 minutes** | Baking time: **7 minutes** | **12 servings**

  1 (1-pound) loaf (12 slices) sliced dark pumpernickel or rye bread*
  4 (1-ounce) slices LAND O LAKES® Deli Swiss Cheese
  ½ cup LAND O LAKES® Butter, melted
  1 teaspoon garlic salt
24 strips (1½ to 2 inches long) roasted red pepper

• Heat oven to 350°F. Cut off crust from each slice of bread with kitchen shears or knife, shaping slice into an oval resembling a football.

• Cut 2 slices cheese into 6 (4×⅝-inch) strips each (12 strips). Cut remaining 2 slices cheese into 12 (2×⅝-inch) strips each (24 strips).

• Combine melted butter and garlic salt in small bowl. Place bread slices onto large ungreased baking sheet. Brush slices with half of butter mixture. Bake for 4 to 6 minutes or until toasted. Turn slices over; brush with remaining butter mixture.

• To make football design, place 1 long cheese strip in center of bread. Place 2 short cheese strips across long cheese strip. Curve 1 slice red pepper on each end of bread about ¼ inch from end. Repeat with remaining ingredients.

• Bake for 3 to 4 minutes or until cheese just starts to melt. Serve warm.

*Substitute 12 slices whole grain wheat bread.

Greek-Style Chicken Drummies with Cucumber Sauce

Preparation time: **15 minutes** | Baking time: **50 minutes** | 24 drumettes; 2½ cups sauce

Marinade
- ⅔ cup olive oil
- 2 tablespoons lemon juice
- 2 tablespoons finely chopped fresh garlic
- 2 teaspoons dried oregano leaves
- 2 teaspoons salt
- ½ teaspoon coarse ground pepper
- ¼ teaspoon crushed red pepper

Chicken Wings
- 1 (48-ounce) package (22 to 27) frozen chicken wing drumettes, thawed

Cucumber Sauce
- 1 cup plain yogurt
- 1 cup LAND O LAKES® Sour Cream
- 1 small (½ cup) cucumber, peeled, seeded, shredded
- 1 tablespoon lemon juice
- 1 tablespoon dried dill weed
- ½ teaspoon salt
- ¼ teaspoon coarse ground pepper

• Combine all marinade ingredients in large resealable plastic food bag; add chicken drumettes. Tightly seal bag. Turn bag several times to coat chicken. Place bag in pan. Refrigerate, turning occasionally, 3 hours or overnight.

• Combine all cucumber sauce ingredients in small bowl; mix well. Cover; refrigerate for at least 2 hours.

• Heat oven to 425°F. Remove chicken drumettes from marinade; discard marinade. Arrange chicken on aluminum foil-lined 15×10×1-inch jelly-roll pan. Bake for 50 to 55 minutes or until chicken is no longer pink, turning once.

• Serve hot chicken wing drumettes with cucumber sauce.

tip:
Cucumber sauce flavor is best when made a day ahead.

tip:
Chicken wings can be kept warm for entertaining by placing fully baked wings and all remaining juice into slow cooker set on Low heat setting.

Mini Barbecued Beef Sandwiches

Preparation time: **15 minutes** | Cooking time: **4 hours** | **20 mini sandwiches**

Meat
3- to 4-pound chuck roast

Sauce
1½ cups ketchup

1 (1¼-ounce) package onion soup mix

1 tablespoon chili powder

3 tablespoons vinegar

2 tablespoons Worcestershire sauce

2 teaspoons prepared mustard

¼ teaspoon garlic powder

Buns
20 small sandwich buns, split

5 ounces (1¼ cups) LAND O LAKES® Co-Jack®, Chedarella® or Cheddar Cheese, shredded

• Trim fat from meat. Place meat in slow cooker; cut to fit, if necessary.

• Stir together all sauce ingredients in medium bowl; pour over meat. Cover; cook on Low heat setting for 8 to 10 hours, or on High heat setting for 4 to 5 hours or until fork tender.

• Remove meat from sauce. Shred meat. Return meat to sauce.

• To serve, divide meat evenly among buns; sprinkle each sandwich with cheese.

Easy Chili Bean Dip

Preparation time: **5 minutes** | Cooking time: **8 minutes** | 2½ cups

   ½ cup medium or hot picante sauce
   8 ounces (2 cups) LAND O LAKES® Deli American Cheese, shredded
   1 (15-ounce) can black beans, rinsed, drained
   1 (4-ounce) can mild or hot chopped green chiles, drained

      Tortilla chips

• Combine all ingredients except tortilla chips in 2-quart saucepan. Cook over low heat, stirring constantly, until cheese is melted (8 to 10 minutes).

• Serve warm with tortilla chips.

tip:
A small electric slow cooker makes a great serving container and keeps the dip warm. Keep it set on the Low heat setting.

Onion & Garlic Crostini, p. 30

Caramelized Almonds
(opposite page), p. 38

APPETIZER
BUFFET

Plan a sophisticated but simple-to-prepare spread for a night at home for the grown-ups with these easy and elegant foods for small plates.

Pear & Gorgonzola Focaccia

Preparation time: **25 minutes** | Baking time: **17 minutes** | **12 wedges**

- 1 (1 pound) loaf frozen white bread dough, thawed
- 3 tablespoons LAND O LAKES® Butter, melted
- 1 large (1½ cups) ripe pear, cored, sliced*
- 1 tablespoon sugar
- ⅓ cup chopped red bell pepper
- 1 tablespoon chopped fresh rosemary
- 4 ounces Gorgonzola or blue cheese, crumbled

• Grease 12-inch pizza pan. Press bread dough into prepared pan, forming a ridge around edge of pan. Brush with 1 tablespoon butter. Let rise in warm place until doubled in size (20 minutes).

• Meanwhile, melt remaining butter in heavy 10-inch skillet until sizzling; add pear slices. Cook over medium heat 3 minutes, gently turning occasionally. Sprinkle with sugar. Continue cooking until pears are tender (4 to 6 minutes).

• Heat oven to 400°F. Place pears over dough; sprinkle with red pepper and rosemary. Bake for 15 to 20 minutes or until crust is deep golden brown. Sprinkle with Gorgonzola; continue baking until cheese begins to melt (2 to 3 minutes). Serve hot or warm.

*Substitute 1 large (1½ cups) apple, cored, sliced.

tip:
Gorgonzola is Italy's version of blue cheese, made with cow's milk. The cheese is inoculated with Penicillium mold to create the blue-green veins in a creamy, golden cheese. When it is young, Gorgonzola is creamy and smooth, but becomes sharper in flavor and drier in texture as it ages.

Onion & Garlic Crostini

Preparation time: **20 minutes** | Baking time: **10 minutes** | **32 slices**

  1 tablespoon LAND O LAKES® Butter
  3 large (3 cups) onions, finely chopped
  1 tablespoon finely chopped fresh garlic
  ¼ cup thinly sliced green onions
  ¼ pound (½-inch thick) slice LAND O LAKES® Deli Swiss Cheese, shredded
  ¼ teaspoon salt
  1 pound French bread baguette, cut into 32 (½-inch) slices

• Melt butter in 10-inch skillet until sizzling; add 3 cups onions and garlic. Cook over medium heat, stirring occasionally, until onions are softened and golden (8 to 10 minutes). Remove from heat; cool 15 minutes.

• Heat oven to 350°F. Combine green onions, cheese and salt in medium bowl. Add cooled onion mixture; mix well.

• Place bread slices onto ungreased baking sheet. Bake for 4 minutes. Spread about 2 teaspoons onion mixture onto each bread slice. Continue baking for 6 minutes or until cheese is melted.

Marinated Cheese with Peppers & Olives

Preparation time: **20 minutes** | Chilling time: **4 hours** | 6 servings

- ¼ cup olive or vegetable oil
- 12 ounces (about 2 cups) LAND O LAKES® Chedarella® or Cheddar Cheese, cut into ¾-inch cubes
- 2 red bell peppers, cut into ¾-inch pieces*
- 1 (14-ounce) can whole pitted ripe olives, drained
- 1 tablespoon white vinegar
- ½ teaspoon dried basil leaves
- ½ teaspoon dried oregano leaves
- ½ teaspoon finely chopped fresh garlic

• Combine all ingredients in medium bowl. Cover; refrigerate at least 4 hours or overnight.

*Substitute 2 roasted red bell peppers.

Cheddar Pita Crisps

Preparation time: **10 minutes** | Baking time: **12 minutes** | **24 appetizers**

- ½ cup low-fat mayonnaise
- ¼ cup thinly sliced green onions
- 8 ounces (2 cups) LAND O LAKES® Cheddar Cheese, shredded
- ⅛ teaspoon ground red pepper
- 1 (2-ounce) jar diced pimientos, drained
- 4 (7-inch) pita breads

• Heat oven to 350°F. Combine all ingredients except pita breads in medium bowl. Set aside.

• Cut each pita bread into 6 wedges; place onto ungreased baking sheets. Bake for 6 to 7 minutes or until lightly browned.

• Spread wedges with cheese mixture. Continue baking for 6 to 8 minutes or until edges are lightly browned.

Cocktail Grilled Cheese Appetizers

Preparation time: **20 minutes** | Baking time: **10 minutes** | **42 appetizers**

   1 (1 pound) package (42 slices) sliced cocktail sourdough or rye bread
   ¼ cup LAND O LAKES® Butter, softened
   ¼ cup Dijon-style mustard*
   6 ounces (1½ cups) LAND O LAKES® Co-Jack®, Chedarella®, Monterey Jack or Hot Pepper Jack
       Cheese, shredded

• Heat oven to 400°F. Lightly spread 1 side of each bread slice with about ¼ teaspoon butter. Place half of bread slices onto aluminum foil-lined baking sheets, buttered-side down. Top each with about ½ teaspoon mustard, 1 tablespoon cheese and 1 bread slice, buttered-side up.

• Bake, turning once, for 10 to 13 minutes or until golden brown and cheese is melted. Cut each sandwich in half. Serve immediately.

*Substitute honey mustard, orange marmalade, apple butter, cranberry relish, prepared basil pesto or herbed tomato paste.

tip:
Assemble sandwiches ahead on aluminum foil-lined baking sheets; cover with plastic food wrap. Refrigerate up to 4 hours. Bake as directed.

Rustic Vegetable Tart

Preparation time: **30 minutes** | Baking time: **21 minutes** | 8 servings

Pastry

- 1 cup all-purpose flour
- ½ cup cold LAND O LAKES® Butter
- 2 to 3 tablespoons cold water

Filling

- 1 tablespoon olive oil
- ⅓ cup chopped sun-dried tomatoes in oil
- 1 small (1 cup) zucchini, cut into julienne strips
- 1 small orange or yellow bell pepper, cut into thin strips
- 1 teaspoon finely chopped fresh garlic
- ½ cup chopped fresh basil leaves*
- ⅓ cup chopped pitted kalamata olives
- 4 ounces (1 cup) crumbled feta cheese
- 2 tablespoons pine nuts

• Heat oven to 450°F. Place flour in large bowl; cut in butter until mixture resembles coarse crumbs. Mix in enough cold water with fork until flour is moistened. Shape into ball.

• Roll out pastry on lightly floured surface into 12-inch circle. Place into ungreased 9- or 10-inch tart pan with removable bottom or pie pan. Press firmly onto bottom and up side of pan. Cut away excess pastry; prick all over with fork. Bake for 11 to 14 minutes or until golden brown.

• Meanwhile, heat oil in 10-inch skillet until hot; add tomatoes, zucchini, bell pepper and garlic. Cook over medium-high heat, stirring occasionally, until vegetables are tender and liquid is evaporated (5 to 6 minutes). Stir in basil and olives.

• Spoon tomato mixture evenly into baked pastry shell; sprinkle with cheese and pine nuts. Bake for 10 to 12 minutes or until filling is hot and cheese is melted. Let stand 5 minutes before serving. Cut into wedges. Serve warm or cold. Cover; store refrigerated.

*Substitute 2 teaspoons dried basil leaves.

Blue Cheese Appetizer Tart

Preparation time: **30 minutes** | Baking time: **37 minutes** | **16 servings**

Pastry

1½ cups all-purpose flour
½ cup cold LAND O LAKES® Butter
5 to 6 tablespoons cold water

Filling

1 (8-ounce) package cream cheese, softened
⅓ cup crumbled blue cheese
¼ cup LAND O LAKES™ Heavy Whipping Cream
1 egg, slightly beaten
¼ teaspoon coarse ground pepper
⅓ cup chopped roasted red bell peppers
3 tablespoons lightly toasted pine nuts or your favorite chopped nuts
2 tablespoons chopped fresh parsley

• Heat oven to 375°F. Place flour in large bowl; cut in butter with pastry blender or fork until mixture resembles coarse crumbs. Stir in enough cold water with fork until flour mixture is just moistened. Shape into ball.

• Roll out pastry on lightly floured surface to 12-inch circle. Place into ungreased 9- or 10-inch tart pan with removable bottom or pie pan. Press firmly on bottom and up sides of pan. Cut away excess pastry; prick all over with fork. Bake for 17 to 22 minutes or until very lightly browned.

• Meanwhile, combine cream cheese and blue cheese in large bowl. Beat at medium speed, scraping bowl often, until creamy. Continue beating, gradually adding whipping cream, egg and ground pepper until blended. Spread into baked pastry shell. Sprinkle with roasted red pepper, pine nuts and parsley.

• Bake for 20 to 25 minutes or until filling is set. Let stand 20 minutes before serving. To serve, cut into wedges. Cover; store refrigerated.

tip:

To toast pine nuts, spread evenly on shallow baking pan. Bake at 325°F. for 5 to 7 minutes, stirring occasionally, just until lightly browned.

Caramelized Almonds

Preparation time: **5 minutes** | Cooking time: **4 minutes** | **8 servings**

 2 tablespoons LAND O LAKES® Butter
 1 cup slivered almonds
 6 tablespoons sugar

• Melt butter in 10-inch skillet until sizzling; add almonds and 4 tablespoons sugar. Cook over medium heat, stirring constantly, until sugar melts and nuts are golden brown (4 to 5 minutes). (Watch closely to prevent burning.) Remove from heat; stir in remaining 2 tablespoons sugar.

• Quickly spread onto waxed paper; cool completely. Break clusters of nuts into pieces. Store in tightly covered container.

tip:
Almonds brown quickly even after cooking if left in skillet. Therefore, it is important to cool them immediately on waxed paper.

Savory Snack Mix

Preparation time: **10 minutes** | Baking time: **20 minutes** | **24 servings**

    5 cups corn, rice or wheat cereal squares
    2 cups oyster crackers
    2 cups pretzel sticks, broken in half
 1½ cups sweetened dried cranberries
    1 (9.5-ounce) can (2 cups) salted cashew halves
  ½ cup LAND O LAKES® Butter, melted
    1 (1.2-ounce) package Caesar or Italian dry salad dressing mix

• Heat oven to 300°F. Combine all ingredients except butter and salad dressing mix in ungreased large roasting pan.

• Combine butter and salad dressing mix in small bowl. Pour over cereal mixture; toss to coat.

• Bake for 20 to 30 minutes, stirring twice, until lightly browned. Cool completely. Store in container with tight-fitting lid.

tip:
Snack may be baked in two 13×9-inch baking pans or two 15×10×1-inch jelly-roll pans.

Shrimp & Crab Potato Bites

Preparation time: **10 minutes** | Baking time: **30 minutes** | **16 servings**

Potato Crust

1½ cups refrigerated hash brown potatoes

2 tablespoons LAND O LAKES® Butter, melted

Filling

1 (8-ounce) container chive and onion flavored cream cheese

4 ounces (1 cup) LAND O LAKES® Swiss Cheese, shredded

1 (6-ounce) can crabmeat, drained, cartilage removed, flaked

1 (4-ounce) package frozen cooked salad shrimp, thawed, drained

1 egg

1 tablespoon all-purpose flour

⅛ teaspoon ground red pepper

Garnish

Italian parsley leaves, if desired

Salad shrimp, if desired

• Heat oven to 425°F. Combine all crust ingredients in small bowl. Press into bottom of ungreased 8-inch square baking pan. Bake for 20 minutes.

• Meanwhile, combine all filling ingredients except ¼ cup cheese in medium bowl; mix well. Spread mixture over hot, partially baked potato layer. Bake for 10 to 15 minutes or until cheese mixture is set. Let stand 5 minutes. Sprinkle with remaining cheese. Garnish each piece with parsley and shrimp, if desired. Serve warm or at room temperature.

tip:

There is a difference between frozen and canned shrimp. We've selected frozen shrimp for its fresher flavor. Canned shrimp will work just fine, but it has more of a briny flavor than the frozen variety.

Shrimp Appetizer Squares

Preparation time: **20 minutes** | Baking time: **13 minutes** | **20 servings**

    1 (10-ounce) can refrigerated pizza crust dough
    2 tablespoons LAND O LAKES® Butter
    ½ cup chopped green bell pepper
    ½ cup chopped red bell pepper
    1 (6-ounce) package frozen cooked small shrimp
    1 medium onion, sliced into thin rings
    1 teaspoon dried basil leaves
    1 teaspoon finely chopped fresh garlic
    6 ounces (1½ cups) LAND O LAKES® Chedarella® Cheese, shredded

• Heat oven to 425°F. Press dough into 13×9-inch rectangle on greased baking sheet. Bake for 5 to 10 minutes or until light golden brown.

• Melt butter in 10-inch skillet until sizzling; add all remaining ingredients except cheese. Cook over medium heat, stirring occasionally, until vegetables are crisply tender (3 to 4 minutes). Drain.

• Top baked crust with half of cheese. Spoon shrimp and vegetable mixture evenly over cheese; top with remaining cheese. Continue baking for 8 to 10 minutes or until cheese is melted.

Blue Cheese Bruschetta

Preparation time: **15 minutes** | Baking time: **13 minutes** | **12 appetizers**

  12 (½-inch-thick) slices baguette-style French bread
   2 tablespoons LAND O LAKES® Butter, softened
   2 ounces (½ cup) crumbled blue cheese
   1 teaspoon finely chopped fresh chives or green onions
      Dash ground red pepper
  ¼ cup finely chopped red and/or yellow bell pepper*
   1 tablespoon finely chopped fresh parsley

• Heat oven to 400°F. Spread 1 side of bread slices with 1 tablespoon butter. Place onto ungreased baking sheet, buttered-side up. Bake for 8 to 10 minutes or until edges are golden brown. Cool slightly.

• Meanwhile, combine remaining butter, blue cheese, chives and ground red pepper in small bowl; mix well.

• Turn bread slices over. Spread unbuttered sides evenly with blue cheese mixture; sprinkle with bell pepper. Bake for 5 to 6 minutes or until cheese mixture begins to melt. Sprinkle with parsley. Serve warm.

*Substitute ¼ cup finely chopped walnuts.

tip:

For easy entertaining, prepare toasted bread slices and cheese mixture early in the day of your get-together. Store toasted bread slices in a tightly covered container at room temperature and cheese mixture covered in the refrigerator. When ready to prepare appetizers, let cheese mixture come to room temperature for easier spreading.

Gourmet Pizzettas

Preparation time: **30 minutes** | Baking time: **6 minutes** | **32 appetizers**

1	teaspoon LAND O LAKES® Butter
2½	cups fresh spinach leaves, stems removed
1	teaspoon water
4	(6-inch) pita breads
½	cup prepared basil pesto
1	cup cooked bay shrimp, coarsely chopped, if desired
⅓	cup thinly sliced red onion
¼	cup crumbled feta cheese
1	(8-ounce) package (2 cups) LAND O LAKES® Monterey Jack Cheese, shredded

• Heat oven to 425°F. Melt butter in 10-inch skillet over medium-high heat. Add spinach and water. Cover; cook until spinach is wilted (1 to 2 minutes). Remove from heat; stir.

• Spread 1 side of each pita with 2 tablespoons pesto. Place onto ungreased baking sheet, pesto-side up. Top each with ¼ cup shrimp, if desired, ¼ cooked spinach, ¼ onion, 1 tablespoon feta cheese and ½ cup Monterey Jack cheese.

• Bake for 6 to 8 minutes or until cheeses are melted. Cut each pizzetta into 8 wedges. Serve warm.

tip

Assemble pizzettas ahead and wrap in plastic food wrap. Bake just before serving.

Feta Cheesecake, p. 51
Warm Spinach Dip *(opposite page)*, p. 58

SPREADS
AND BREADS

Fresh, savory crackers and breads are no more complicated
to make at home than your favorite cookie recipes are.
Combine them with one or more of the accompanying recipes
for cheesy dips or spreads and you've got the perfect start to
any meal.

Artichoke-Olive Focaccia

Preparation time: **1 hour** | Baking time: **30 minutes** | **12 servings**

Bread

3 to 3½ cups all-purpose or bread flour
1 (¼-ounce) package active dry yeast
1 tablespoon sugar
1 teaspoon salt
1 cup water
3 tablespoons LAND O LAKES® Butter
2 teaspoons finely chopped fresh garlic

Topping

1 tablespoon LAND O LAKES® Butter, melted
1 (6-ounce) jar marinated artichoke hearts, drained, cut large pieces in half
¼ cup sliced ripe olives
¼ cup roasted red pepper strips
½ cup shredded Parmesan cheese

LAND O LAKES® Butter, melted, if desired

• Combine 1½ cups flour, yeast, sugar and salt in large bowl. Set aside.

• Combine water, 3 tablespoons butter and garlic in 1-quart saucepan. Cook over medium heat, stirring occasionally, until mixture reaches 120°F. to 130°F. (2 to 4 minutes). (Butter may not melt completely.) Add warm butter mixture to flour mixture. Beat at low speed until flour is moistened. Increase speed to medium; beat, scraping bowl often, until smooth. Stir in enough remaining flour until dough forms a ball and leaves sides of bowl.

• Turn dough onto lightly floured surface; knead until smooth and elastic (3 to 5 minutes), adding more flour as needed to prevent sticking.

• Press dough into 10-inch circle on greased baking sheet. Cover loosely with plastic food wrap; let rise in warm place until double in size (45 to 60 minutes).

• Heat oven to 375°F. Make indentations (about 1-inch deep) 2 inches apart in dough with floured finger or handle of wooden spoon. Brush dough with 1 tablespoon melted butter. Sprinkle artichokes, olives, red pepper strips and Parmesan cheese evenly over dough; press large pieces into dough.

• Bake for 30 to 35 minutes or until edges are golden brown. Brush with melted butter, if desired. Cut into wedges. Serve warm or cool.

Cheddar Pecan Roll

Preparation time: **10 minutes** | Chilling time: **3 hours** | **40 appetizer slices**

> ¼ cup LAND O LAKES® Sour Cream
> 6 ounces (1½ cups) LAND O LAKES® Cheddar Cheese,
>   shredded
> ¼ cup finely chopped pecans, toasted
>
>   Assorted fresh fruit, if desired

• Combine sour cream and cheese in large bowl. Beat at medium speed, scraping bowl often, until well mixed. Stir in pecans.

• Shape mixture into 10×1¼-inch roll. Wrap in plastic food wrap. Refrigerate until firm (3 to 4 hours).

• To serve, slice into ¼-inch slices. Arrange on large platter with assorted fresh fruit, if desired.

tip:
Cheese will blend more easily with other ingredients if at room temperature. Shred cheese when cold; let stand about 15 minutes.

tip:
Fruits that complement Cheddar Pecan Roll are strawberries, cherries, red and green grapes, sliced apples and pears.

Apricot-Cashew-Pepper Cheese Torta

Preparation time: **15 minutes** | Chilling time: **2 hours** | **2½ cups**

- 8 ounces (2 cups) LAND O LAKES® Cheddar Cheese, shredded
- 2 (8-ounce) packages cream cheese, softened
- 2 tablespoons milk
- 1 teaspoon onion powder
- ⅓ cup chopped dried apricots*
- ⅓ cup chopped red bell pepper
- ⅓ cup coarsely chopped cashews

  Baguette slices or pita bread wedges, if desired

• Combine Cheddar cheese, cream cheese, milk and onion powder in small bowl. Beat at medium speed, scraping bowl often, until well mixed.

• Spread one-third cheese mixture onto bottom of 9-inch round serving dish; sprinkle evenly with dried apricots. Spread one-third cheese mixture carefully over apricots; sprinkle with bell pepper. Repeat with remaining cheese mixture and cashews. Sprinkle with additional apricots and bell pepper, if desired.

• Cover; refrigerate at least 2 hours to blend flavors. Remove from refrigerator 30 minutes before serving. Store refrigerated. Serve with baguette slices, if desired.

*Substitute chopped dried peaches or fruit bits.

tip:
To soften 1 (8-ounce) package cream cheese in the microwave, remove foil wrapper. Place on microwave-safe plate; microwave uncovered on MEDIUM (50% power) for 1 to 1½ minutes.

Pepper, Olive & Cheese Spread

Preparation time: **30 minutes** | **2 cups**

   ½ cup freshly grated Parmesan cheese
   4 ounces (1 cup) LAND O LAKES® Mozzarella Cheese, shredded
   1 (8-ounce) package cream cheese, softened
   2 tablespoons finely chopped fresh parsley, rosemary and/or thyme leaves
   ½ teaspoon coarsely ground pepper
   ⅓ cup roasted red bell pepper pasta or spaghetti sauce
   ⅓ cup chopped pitted kalamata olives
      Chopped parsley, if desired
      Fresh rosemary sprigs, if desired

      Crusty bread slices or crackers

• Combine Parmesan cheese, mozzarella cheese, cream cheese, herbs and pepper in large bowl.

• Spread cheese mixture into 6-inch circle on 9-inch serving plate. Cover; refrigerate until serving time.

• Just before serving, spread pasta sauce over cheese mixture, leaving ½ inch around edge. Top with chopped olives. Garnish with parsley and rosemary, if desired.

• Serve with crusty bread or crackers.

Feta Cheesecake *(photo on page 44)*

Preparation time: **30 minutes** | Baking time: **35 minutes** | **32 servings**

Crust

- 1⅓ cups (about 35) sesame seed cracker crumbs
- ¼ cup shredded Parmesan cheese
- ⅓ cup LAND O LAKES® Butter, melted

Filling

- 2 (8-ounce) packages cream cheese, softened
- 2 (4-ounce) packages crumbled feta cheese with basil and tomato
- 3 eggs
- 1 (4¼-ounce) can (½ cup) chopped pitted ripe olives, well-drained
- ⅓ cup sliced green onions
- 1 teaspoon dried oregano leaves
- ½ teaspoon coarse ground pepper
- ¼ teaspoon garlic salt

Topping

- 2 medium Roma tomatoes, finely chopped
- ⅓ cup sliced green onions

Sesame seed or rye crackers, if desired

• Heat oven to 325°F. Combine all crust ingredients in medium bowl. Press onto bottom and 1½ inches up sides of ungreased 9-inch springform pan or aluminum foil-lined 9-inch round baking pan, leaving a 1-inch overhang.

• Combine cream cheese and feta cheese in large bowl. Beat at medium speed, scraping bowl often, until creamy. Add eggs, beating just until combined. Stir in all remaining filling ingredients. Pour into crust. Bake for 35 to 40 minutes or until just set 3 inches from edge of pan. Cool 15 minutes; loosen sides of springform pan. Cool on wire rack for 2 hours. Loosely cover; refrigerate at least 2 hours.

• To serve, cut into wedges. Top each wedge with tomato and green onions. Serve with crackers, if desired. Store refrigerated.

tip:

Check cheesecake at the minimum time for doneness by gently shaking the pan. If the center still jiggles and the edges appear firm, the cheesecake is done. The cheesecake will continue to set as it cools.

Flax Seed Cracker Bread

Preparation time: **20 minutes** | Baking time: **12 minutes** | **5½ dozen pieces**

> 1 cup whole wheat flour
> ½ cup all-purpose flour
> 2 tablespoons sugar
> 1 teaspoon baking powder
> ½ teaspoon baking soda
> ½ teaspoon salt
> ¼ cup LAND O LAKES® Butter, softened
> ½ cup buttermilk*
> 3 tablespoons flax seed or sesame seed

• Heat oven to 375°F. Combine whole wheat flour, flour, sugar, baking powder, baking soda and salt in large bowl. Cut in butter with pastry blender or fork just until mixture resembles coarse crumbs. Add buttermilk; stir just until flour is moistened. Stir in flax seed.

• Place dough on lightly floured surface; knead 3 to 5 times until smooth. Divide dough in half. Roll out each half with floured rolling pin or pat each half with floured fingers into 13×11-inch rectangle on greased baking sheets. Prick all over with fork.

• Bake for 12 to 15 minutes or until golden brown. Cool completely. Break into pieces.

*Substitute 1½ teaspoons vinegar or lemon juice and enough milk to equal ½ cup. Let stand 10 minutes.

tip:
Varying shades of brown are typical of cracker bread. Try to roll or press dough out very evenly for even browning.

tip:
Flax seeds, when used as whole seeds, add texture to foods. Ground seeds give the most nutritional benefit and are a primary source of Omega-3 and Omega-6 fatty acids. Flax seed is available in the health food section of the supermarket.

Mediterranean Olive Tapenade

Preparation time: **30 minutes** | Baking time: **4 minutes** | **44 cheese chips; 1 cup tapenade**

Tapenade

½ cup chopped stuffed green or salad olives

¼ cup chopped black olives

¼ cup chopped kalamata olives

2 tablespoons chopped fresh cilantro

1 tablespoon white wine vinegar

2 teaspoons capers, rinsed, drained

2 teaspoons finely chopped fresh garlic

1 teaspoon honey

¼ teaspoon chopped jalapeño or serrano chile peppers

½ teaspoon balsamic vinegar

1½ teaspoons fresh basil leaves*

• Combine all tapenade ingredients in small bowl; mix well. Cover; let stand at room temperature to blend flavors (30 to 60 minutes).

• Heat oven to 350°F. Place cheese cubes in pairs, 4 inches apart, onto nonstick baking sheets. Bake for 4 to 5 minutes or until cheese is lacy in appearance and lightly browned on edges. Cool on baking sheets until cheese stops sizzling (1 minute). Carefully remove with spatula onto paper towels. Cool completely.

• To serve, drain any liquid from tapenade mixture. Spoon onto cheese chips. Garnish with fresh basil leaves, if desired.

*Substitute ½ teaspoon dried basil leaves.

tip:

Use leftover olive mixture on crackers, pita bread or sandwiches.

Cheese Chips

8 ounces LAND O LAKES® Monterey Jack Cheese, cut into ½-inch cubes

Fresh basil leaves, if desired

Taco Cheese Spread

Preparation time: **10 minutes** | **2¾ cups**

   ½ cup LAND O LAKES® Sour Cream
  12 ounces (3 cups) LAND O LAKES® Cheddar Cheese, shredded
   1 (3-ounce) package cream cheese, softened
   ¼ cup sliced pitted ripe olives, drained
   2 tablespoons chopped green chiles
   1 tablespoon taco seasoning mix

      Fresh cilantro leaves
      Crackers or tortilla chips
      Fresh vegetable dippers, if desired

• Combine sour cream, Cheddar cheese and cream cheese in large bowl. Beat at medium speed until well mixed. Add olives, chiles and seasoning mix; continue beating until well mixed.

• Place cheese mixture into serving bowl. Cover; refrigerate at least 30 minutes to blend flavors.

• Garnish with cilantro. Serve with crackers or vegetable dippers, if desired.

Cheddar Shortbread Bites

Preparation time: **20 minutes** | Baking time: **12 minutes** | **60 appetizers**

Shortbread

1 cup all-purpose flour
½ cup LAND O LAKES® Butter, softened
½ teaspoon salt
   Dash ground red pepper
8 ounces (2 cups) LAND O LAKES® Sharp
   Cheddar Cheese, shredded

Topping

2 tablespoons poppy seed
2 tablespoons sesame seed
1 egg white
1 tablespoon water

• Combine flour, butter, salt and red pepper in medium bowl; beat at medium speed until dough forms. Add cheese; mix until ball forms. Shape dough into 8-inch ball; flatten slightly. Wrap in plastic food wrap; refrigerate 2 hours or overnight.

• Heat oven to 350°F. Roll out dough on lightly floured surface to ¼-inch thickness. (It will be hard to roll at first, but will soften. Press together any cracks that form on edges of dough.) Cut dough with 1½-inch cookie cutters or pizza cutter into desired shapes (squares, triangles, circles). Place onto ungreased baking sheets.

• Combine poppy seed and sesame seed in small bowl. Beat egg white and water in another small bowl. Brush cut-outs with egg white mixture; sprinkle with seed mixture.

• Bake for 12 to 15 minutes or until very lightly browned around edges. Immediately loosen from baking sheets; cool on baking sheets.

tip:
Lining baking sheets with kitchen parchment paper makes shortbread easier to remove and clean-up faster.

tip:
Shortbread can be topped with a variety of other ingredients, such as chili powder, seasoned salt, fennel seed or herbs.

Four Cheese & Walnut Cheese Ball

Preparation time: **30 minutes** | Chilling time: **3 hours** | **2½ cups**

Cheese Ball

- 4 ounces (1 cup) LAND O LAKES® Cheddar Cheese, shredded
- 1 (8-ounce) container sharp Cheddar cold pack cheese
- 1 (8-ounce) package cream cheese, softened
- 1 (4-ounce) package blue cheese, crumbled
- ¾ teaspoon dried dill weed
- ½ teaspoon dried basil leaves
- ½ teaspoon celery salt
- ½ teaspoon Italian seasoning*
- 2 teaspoons finely chopped fresh garlic
- 1 tablespoon soy sauce
- ½ cup chopped walnuts, toasted
- ¼ cup chopped fresh parsley

Dippers

Crackers or baked pita bread wedges
Apple slices

• Combine all cheese ball ingredients except walnuts and parsley in large bowl. Beat at low speed, scraping bowl often, until well mixed. Cover; refrigerate until firm (at least 3 hours or overnight).

• Combine walnuts and parsley in small bowl. Shape cheese mixture into ball; roll in walnut mixture to coat. Serve with crackers or apple slices.

*Substitute ⅛ teaspoon each dried oregano leaves, dried marjoram leaves and dried basil leaves, and 1⁄16 teaspoon rubbed sage.

Coconut Orange Fruit Dip

Preparation time: **10 minutes** | Chilling time: **1 hour** | **2 cups**

Dip

2 cups LAND O LAKES® Sour Cream
½ cup powdered sugar
⅛ teaspoon ground allspice
¼ cup sweetened flaked coconut, toasted
2 teaspoons freshly grated orange peel

Toasted coconut, if desired

Dippers

Strawberries, pineapple, apple and/or peach slices, as desired

• Combine sour cream, sugar and allspice in medium bowl with wire whisk until smooth. Stir in ¼ cup coconut and orange peel. Cover; refrigerate to blend flavors (1 hour).

• Garnish with additional toasted coconut, if desired. Serve with desired fresh fruit.

tip:
To toast coconut, spread coconut in single layer on ungreased 15×10×1-inch jelly-roll pan. Bake at 350°F., stirring occasionally, for 5 to 7 minutes or until lightly browned.

tip:
Dip can be made two to three days ahead. Keep refrigerated.

Warm Spinach Dip

Preparation time: **15 minutes** | Cooking time: **8 minutes** | **4 cups**

¼ cup LAND O LAKES® Butter
1 large (1 cup) onion, chopped
1 small (½ cup) red bell pepper, chopped
1 tablespoon finely chopped fresh garlic
2 tablespoons all-purpose flour
½ cup chicken broth
½ cup LAND O LAKES™ Heavy Whipping Cream
½ cup feta cheese with garlic and herbs*
¼ cup plain yogurt
1 (10-ounce) package fresh spinach leaves, stems removed, cut into thin strips
⅛ teaspoon hot pepper sauce
   Salt
   Pepper

   Sesame crackers, party rye cocktail bread slices and/or assorted vegetable sticks (such as carrots or celery)

• Melt butter in 10-inch skillet until sizzling; add onion, red pepper and garlic. Cook over medium heat, stirring occasionally, until onion is softened (5 to 6 minutes). Stir in flour; continue cooking 1 minute. Add broth and whipping cream. Continue cooking, stirring with wire whisk, until mixture is thickened (2 to 3 minutes).

• Remove from heat. Stir in cheese, yogurt, spinach and hot pepper sauce. Season with salt and pepper to taste. Serve warm with crackers, bread slices or assorted vegetable sticks.

*Substitute 1 cup freshly shredded Parmesan cheese.

tip:
Dip can also be spooned into a bread bowl.

Nutty Artichoke Spread, p. 66

Mushroom Pinwheels *(opposite page)*, p. 75

EASY CASUAL ENTERTAINING

Satisfying friends and family just got a whole lot easier, thanks to this collection of appetizers and snacks. The broad appeal of these recipes is matched only by the simple steps necessary to create them.

El Paso Tortilla Wheels

Preparation time: **20 minutes** | Chilling time: **8 hours** | **5 dozen appetizers**

  8 ounces (2 cups) LAND O LAKES® Cheddar Cheese, shredded
 ¼ cup sliced green or ripe olives
  1 cup LAND O LAKES® Sour Cream
  1 (4-ounce) can chopped mild green chiles
  1 (3-ounce) package cream cheese, softened
     Garlic powder, if desired
     Hot pepper sauce, if desired

10 (7- to 8-inch) flour tortillas

• Combine all ingredients except tortillas in large bowl.

• Spread ¼ cup cheese mixture onto 1 tortilla. Roll up jelly-roll style; wrap in plastic food wrap. Repeat with remaining cheese mixture and tortillas. Refrigerate at least 8 hours or overnight.

• Slice off ends of tortillas; discard. Slice each tortilla roll into 6 pieces.

Fruit 'n Cheese Dippers

Preparation time: **15 minutes** | Chilling time: **30 minutes** | **8 servings**

Dip

1 cup plain yogurt
2 tablespoons honey

Dippers

4 cups your favorite fresh fruit, cut into 1-inch pieces (apples, strawberries, mandarin orange segments, grapes, pears, pineapple, etc.)

4 ounces LAND O LAKES® Cheddar Cheese, cubed

4 ounces LAND O LAKES® Swiss Cheese, cubed

8 (8-inch) skewers

• Stir together yogurt and honey in small bowl. Cover; refrigerate at least 30 minutes.

• Meanwhile, assemble dippers by alternating fruit pieces and cheese cubes on skewers. Serve with dip.

tip:
Dip cut fruit pieces in lemon juice to prevent discoloration.

Funny Face Pizza Muffins

Preparation time: **15 minutes** | Microwaving time: **45 seconds** | **4 servings**

Muffins

1 cup pizza sauce

4 English muffins, split, toasted

4 ounces (1 cup) LAND O LAKES® Provolone or Mozzarella Cheese, shredded

Toppings

Sliced black olives

Carrot curls or shredded carrots

Green and/or red bell pepper strips

Sliced mushrooms

Cherry tomatoes, halved

• Spread 2 tablespoons pizza sauce on each toasted muffin half; top each with 2 tablespoons cheese.

• Place muffins onto microwave-safe plate; microwave on HIGH for 45 to 60 seconds or until cheese is melted. Place toppings on muffins to create faces.

tip: _____

Use a potato peeler to make carrot curls. Ready-to-eat shredded carrots can be purchased in the produce section of the supermarket.

Nutty Artichoke Spread

Preparation time: **20 minutes** | Baking time: **20 minutes** | 2½ cups

⅔ cup mayonnaise

½ cup finely chopped pecans

1 (8-ounce) package (2 cups) LAND O LAKES® Chedarella® or Cheddar Cheese, shredded

4 slices bacon, crisply cooked, crumbled

1 (14-ounce) can artichoke hearts, drained, quartered

1 tablespoon finely chopped onion

1 tablespoon lemon juice

Sliced artisan bread or crackers

• Heat oven to 350°F. Stir together all ingredients except bread in large bowl. Spoon mixture into ungreased 9-inch ovenproof shallow dish or pie pan.

• Bake for 20 to 25 minutes or until cheese is melted and spread is heated through. Serve with sliced bread or crackers.

Southwestern Quesadillas

Preparation time: **30 minutes** | Baking time: **10 minutes** | 6 servings

Filling

- ⅓ cup mayonnaise
- ⅓ cup LAND O LAKES® Sour Cream
- 4 ounces (1 cup) sliced deli chicken breast, cut into small pieces
- 4 ounces (1 cup) LAND O LAKES® Chedarella® Cheese, shredded
- 2 tablespoons sliced green onions
- 2 tablespoons chopped mild green chiles, drained
- ½ teaspoon freshly grated lime peel
- 3 drops hot pepper sauce

Tortillas

- 6 (8-inch) flour tortillas
- 1 tablespoon LAND O LAKES® Butter, melted
  Ground red pepper or chili powder

Toppings

  LAND O LAKES® Sour Cream
  Salsa

• Heat oven to 375°F. Combine all filling ingredients in large bowl.

• Spread about ⅓ cup filling mixture on half of each tortilla; fold other side of tortilla over cheese mixture. Brush both sides of each tortilla with butter; sprinkle top with red pepper. Place onto ungreased large baking sheet. Repeat with remaining tortillas. Bake for 10 to 15 minutes or until heated through.

• To serve, cut each quesadilla into three wedges. Serve with sour cream and salsa.

Cheese Roll-ups

Preparation time: **15 minutes** | Baking time: **13 minutes** | 12 roll-ups

1 (10-ounce) can refrigerated pizza dough
4 ounces (½ cup) LAND O LAKES® Chedarella® Cheese, shredded

• Heat oven to 350°F. Press dough into 12×8-inch rectangle on lightly floured surface. Sprinkle cheese over crust to within ½ inch of edge. Roll up dough, starting with long edge. Pinch edges to seal.

• Cut roll into 1-inch pieces with sharp knife. Place 2 inches apart onto ungreased nonstick baking sheet. Bake for 13 to 16 minutes or until golden brown.

variations:
Italian-flavored Roll-ups: Prepare dough as directed above. Sprinkle dough with 2 teaspoons Italian seasoning before adding cheese.
Taco-flavored Roll-ups: Prepare dough as directed above. Sprinkle dough with 4 teaspoons taco seasoning before adding cheese. Continue as directed above.

tip:
If you do not have a nonstick baking sheet, use a regular aluminum baking sheet. Grease baking sheet well and remove roll-ups immediately after baking to prevent sticking. Increase baking time by 2 minutes.

Spinach Cheddar Bread Bowl

Preparation time: **20 minutes** | **4 cups dip**

   8 ounces (2 cups) LAND O LAKES® Cheddar Cheese, shredded

1½ cups LAND O LAKES® Sour Cream

   ½ cup mayonnaise

   1 (10-ounce) package frozen chopped spinach, thawed, well-drained

   1 (8-ounce) can water chestnuts, drained, chopped

   1 tablespoon dried onion soup mix

   1 (1-pound) round unsliced loaf rye or sourdough bread

• Combine all ingredients except bread in large bowl; mix well.

• Cut out center of bread, leaving sides and bottom about 1 inch thick. Fill bread bowl with dip; refrigerate until serving time (at least 30 minutes). Cut remaining bread into small pieces to serve with dip.

tip:
Spinach dip can be made a day ahead. Keep refrigerated.

Cheesy Roasted Red Pepper Crostini

Preparation time: **20 minutes** | Broiling time: **4 minutes** | **16 crostini**

¼ cup LAND O LAKES® Butter

2 large cloves fresh garlic, finely chopped

16 (¼-inch) slices Italian bread

8 (1-ounce) slices LAND O LAKES® Deli Provolone Cheese, cut in half

1 (7.25-ounce) jar roasted red peppers, drained, cut into strips

⅔ cup freshly shredded Parmesan or Romano cheese

  Fresh herb sprigs (Italian parsley, tarragon, basil or oregano), if desired

• Heat broiler. Melt butter and garlic in 1-quart saucepan over medium heat until sizzling.

• Place bread onto ungreased baking sheets. Broil 6 inches from heat until bread is lightly toasted (2 to 3 minutes). Turn bread over; brush untoasted side with melted butter mixture. Top each with 1 half slice cheese and about 1 tablespoon roasted red peppers. Sprinkle with Parmesan cheese.

• Continue broiling until cheeses are melted and starting to brown (2 to 3 minutes). Serve warm; garnish with sprig of fresh herb, if desired.

tip:
Bottled roasted red peppers can be found in the condiment section with the olives or sometimes in the deli department of your supermarket.

Cheesy Bacon Snack Bread

Preparation time: **20 minutes** | Baking time: **15 minutes** | **20 servings**

- 1 (1-pound) loaf frozen white bread dough, thawed according to package directions
- 2 tablespoons LAND O LAKES® Butter, melted
- ½ teaspoon onion salt
- ½ teaspoon liquid smoke, if desired
- 1 (8-ounce) package (2 cups) LAND O LAKES® Co-Jack® or Chedarella® Cheese, shredded
- 5 slices (⅓ cup) crisply cooked bacon, crumbled*
- 2 tablespoons chopped fresh parsley or ¼ cup sliced green onions

• Press dough into greased 15×10×1-inch jelly-roll pan or into 15×10×1-inch rectangle on large greased baking sheet.

• Combine melted butter, onion salt and liquid smoke in small bowl. Brush evenly over dough. Cover; let rise in warm place until double in size (45 to 60 minutes).

• Heat oven to 375°F. Prick dough carefully all over with fork. Sprinkle cheese and bacon evenly over dough. Bake for 15 to 20 minutes or until edges of dough are golden brown and cheese starts to brown. Sprinkle with parsley. Cool 10 minutes. Cut into serving pieces. Serve warm.

*Substitute ⅓ cup real bacon bits.

tip:

If thawed dough is cold, let stand, covered, about 30 minutes at room temperature before pressing into pan.

tip:

To reheat snack bread, heat oven to 350°F. Wrap bread in aluminum foil. Bake for 10 to 15 minutes or until heated through.

Triple Cheese Quesadilla Stackers

Preparation time: **15 minutes** | **4 servings**

   6 (7-inch) flour tortillas
   1 (6-ounce) package sliced portabella mushrooms*
   6 ounces LAND O LAKES® Hot Pepper Monterey Jack Cheese, cut into ½-inch strips
  ⅔ cup roasted red peppers, cut into strips
   6 ounces LAND O LAKES® Chedarella® Cheese, cut into ½-inch strips

      LAND O LAKES® Sour Cream

• Place 1 tortilla in 10-inch skillet; layer with 3 ounces mushrooms, 3 ounces Monterey Jack cheese, 1 tortilla, ⅓ cup peppers, 3 ounces Chedarella® cheese and 1 tortilla.

• Cook over medium heat until bottom of tortilla is lightly browned (2 to 3 minutes).

• Turn; continue cooking until tortilla is browned and cheese is melted (2 to 3 minutes). Repeat with remaining ingredients.

• To serve, cut into wedges. Serve with sour cream.

*Substitute sliced button mushrooms.

Italian Nachos

Preparation time: **20 minutes** | Baking time: **5 minutes** | **8 servings**

   1 (10-ounce) container refrigerated four-cheese Alfredo or Alfredo sauce, warmed
  ¼ teaspoon crushed red pepper
  8 ounces white corn tortilla chips
  4 ounces hot Italian sausage, cooked
  4 ounces (1 cup) LAND O LAKES® Mozzarella Cheese, shredded
  ½ cup chopped tomato
  ¼ cup sliced green onions
  1 (2¼-ounce) can sliced pitted ripe olives

• Heat oven to 450°F. Combine cheese sauce and red pepper in small bowl.

• Spread half of tortilla chips on ovenproof platter; top with half cheese sauce, half Italian sausage and half mozzarella cheese. Repeat with remaining chips, cheese sauce, sausage and cheese.

• Bake for 5 minutes or until cheese is melted. Top with remaining ingredients. Serve immediately.

Mushroom Pinwheels

Preparation time: **25 minutes** | Baking time: **15 minutes** | 60 pinwheels

- ¼ cup LAND O LAKES® Butter
- 1 (8-ounce) package sliced fresh mushrooms, finely chopped
- 2 tablespoons all-purpose flour
- ¼ teaspoon salt
- ½ cup LAND O LAKES™ Half & Half
- 1 teaspoon finely chopped fresh dill
- 1 teaspoon lemon juice
- ½ teaspoon garlic or onion salt
- 20 slices soft sandwich bread
- 2 tablespoons LAND O LAKES® Butter, melted

    Fresh dill, if desired

• Heat oven to 400°F. Melt ¼ cup butter in 12-inch skillet until sizzling; add mushrooms. Cook over medium-high heat until mushrooms are softened (about 5 minutes). Stir in flour and salt; mix until well blended. Add half & half; continue cooking, stirring constantly, until mixture is thickened. Stir in 1 teaspoon dill, lemon juice and garlic salt. Pour mushroom mixture into shallow dish. Cover with plastic food wrap; refrigerate until cool and thickened (about 30 minutes).

• Meanwhile, cut crusts from bread. Roll bread slices with rolling pin until very thin. Spread 1 tablespoon mushroom mixture on each slice; roll up. Place rolls onto parchment paper-lined or greased aluminum foil-lined baking sheets, seam-side down. Freeze for 15 minutes.

• Cut rolls into thirds using serrated knife; separate on baking sheets. Brush with melted butter. Bake for 15 to 17 minutes or until golden brown. Serve immediately. Garnish with fresh dill, if desired.

tip:
To make ahead, prepare as directed above except do not cut, brush with butter or bake. Wrap pinwheels in plastic food wrap; place in freezer bag. Freeze for up to 2 weeks. Thaw rolls at room temperature for 30 minutes before slicing. Heat oven to 400°F. Brush with butter and bake as directed above.

Sweet & Savory Snack Mix

Preparation time: **10 minutes** | Baking time: **1 hour** | **8 cups**

    3 cups pretzel sticks
    3 cups honey graham cereal
    2 cups crispy wheat cereal squares
  1½ cups mixed nuts
   ½ cup LAND O LAKES® Butter, melted
    3 tablespoons firmly packed brown sugar
    2 tablespoons Worcestershire sauce

• Heat oven to 250°F. Combine pretzels, honey graham cereal, cereal squares and mixed nuts in ungreased 15×10×1-inch jelly-roll pan.

• Combine butter, brown sugar and Worcestershire sauce in small bowl. Pour over cereal mixture; toss lightly to coat.

• Bake, stirring every 15 minutes, for 1 hour. Cool completely. Store in container with tight-fitting lid.

Tortilla Cracker Bread with Mango Salsa

Preparation time: **20 minutes** | Baking time: **7 minutes** | **32 crackers; 3 cups salsa**

Crackers

- 8 (6-inch) flour tortillas
- 3 tablespoons LAND O LAKES® Butter, melted
- 1 to 2 teaspoons garlic salt with parsley

Salsa

- 1 (16-ounce) jar thick and chunky salsa
- 1 medium (1 cup) mango, peeled, cut into ½-inch cubes
- 1 (8.75-ounce) can whole-kernel corn, well-drained
- ¼ cup chopped green onions

• Heat oven to 375°F. Brush both sides of each tortilla with butter. Sprinkle one side of each tortilla with garlic salt.

• Place tortillas onto 2 large aluminum foil-lined baking sheets. Bake, rotating sheets halfway through baking, for 7 to 9 minutes or until golden brown and crisp. Cool on wire rack.

• Meanwhile, combine all salsa ingredients in small bowl. Break each cooled tortilla into 4 pieces. Serve with salsa.

tip:
To choose a ripe mango, look for fruit that is heavy and soft to the touch. Color is not always the best indicator because there are so many varieties. If a good mango is hard to find, substitute ripe peaches or papaya in the salsa.

tip:
Prepare cracker bread up to two days ahead. Store in a container with a tight-fitting lid.

tip:
The salsa can be prepared a day ahead; keep refrigerated.

easy casual entertaining

Tomato Basil Pizza

Preparation time: **10 minutes** | Baking time: **10 minutes** | **6 servings**

¼ cup nonfat mayonnaise or salad dressing
½ teaspoon purchased minced garlic
1 (10 to 12-ounce) round pre-baked thin Italian pizza crust
¼ cup chopped fresh basil leaves*
4 Roma tomatoes, coarsely chopped
¼ cup grated Parmesan cheese
6 ounces (1½ cups) LAND O LAKES® Mozzarella Cheese, shredded

Chopped fresh basil leaves, if desired

• Heat oven to 425°F. Combine mayonnaise and garlic in small bowl; mix well.

• Place pizza crust onto ungreased baking sheet. Spread mayonnaise mixture to within ½ inch of edge; sprinkle with ¼ cup chopped basil leaves. Top with tomatoes and cheeses.

• Bake for 10 to 12 minutes or until cheese is melted and pizza is heated through. Sprinkle with chopped basil leaves, if desired.

*Substitute 2 teaspoons dried basil leaves.

tip:

Two words describe the best way to store fresh tomatoes—never refrigerate. Refrigerator temperatures can cause tomatoes to become mealy or watery in texture and milder in flavor.

Sun-Dried Tomato Cheese Bread, p. 84

Tomato & Roasted Garlic Tart *(opposite page)*, p. 90

PATIO
PARTY

Wow the crowd at your next backyard gathering. Treat them to appetizers with a new twist. They don't have to know how easy these recipes are to make.

Beef Brochettes with Apricot Sauce

Preparation time: **30 minutes** | Cooking time: **10 minutes** | **16 servings**

Brochettes

  2 pounds (1-inch-thick) boneless beef loin
     top sirloin steak, trimmed, cut into
     2×¼-inch strips
  1 small onion, cut into ½-inch wedges
  8 (10-inch) wooden skewers, soaked in water
     30 minutes*
  ¼ cup LAND O LAKES® Butter, melted
  1 tablespoon finely chopped fresh parsley
  1 clove fresh garlic, finely chopped
  1 teaspoon Dijon-style mustard

Sauce

  1 cup barbecue sauce
  ½ cup apricot preserves
  ¼ cup Dijon-style mustard

• Heat broiler. Alternately thread meat and onion wedges onto skewers. Place onto aluminum foil-lined baking sheet or broiler pan.

• Combine butter, parsley, garlic and 1 teaspoon mustard in small bowl. Brush onto beef and onion. Broil 6 inches from heat, turning once, until desired doneness (10 to 15 minutes).

• Meanwhile, combine all sauce ingredients in medium bowl. Serve at room temperature or warmed with beef.

*Substitute metal skewers.

tip:
Assemble the skewers ahead of time, along with the seasoned butter and sweet-tart barbecue sauce. Refrigerate until serving time.

Cheddar & Bacon Log

Preparation time: **15 minutes** | Chilling time: **4 hours** | **3 cups**

   1 (8-ounce) package cream cheese, softened
   3 tablespoons mayonnaise
   ⅛ teaspoon Worcestershire sauce
   3 to 4 drops hot pepper sauce
   ¼ cup crumbled crisply cooked bacon
   8 ounces (2 cups) LAND O LAKES® Cheddar Cheese, shredded
   2 tablespoons sliced green onions
   1 cup chopped pecans, toasted

   Crackers

• Combine cream cheese, mayonnaise, Worcestershire sauce and hot pepper sauce in large bowl. Beat at medium speed, scraping bowl often, until smooth. Stir in bacon, cheese and green onions by hand. Cover; refrigerate at least 2 hours.

• Form cheese mixture into log shape or cheese ball; roll in pecans to coat. Wrap in plastic food wrap; refrigerate until well chilled (at least 2 hours). Serve with crackers.

Sun-Dried Tomato Cheese Bread

Preparation time: **20 minutes** | Grilling time: **5 minutes** | **8 servings**

  1 (1-pound) loaf French bread
  ½ cup LAND O LAKES® Butter, softened
  2 tablespoons sun-dried tomato spread or finely chopped oil-packed sun-dried tomatoes, drained
  ½ teaspoon garlic powder
  8 ounces (2 cups) LAND O LAKES® Mozzarella Cheese, shredded
  ¼ cup grated Parmesan cheese

• Heat gas grill on medium-low or charcoal grill until coals are ash white. Slice bread loaf in half lengthwise.

• Combine butter, sun-dried tomato spread and garlic powder in small bowl.

• Evenly spread cut sides of bread halves with butter mixture; top with cheeses.

• Place bread halves onto grill, crust-side down. Close lid; grill until cheeses are melted (3 to 7 minutes). Slice each bread half into 8 pieces.

tip:
Make use of the upper rack if your grill has one. Time for grilling will vary depending on your grill.

Grilled Cracker Crust Pizzas

Preparation time: **20 minutes** | Grilling time: **3 minutes** | **4 pizzas**

   4 (8-inch) flour tortillas
   2 teaspoons LAND O LAKES® Butter, melted
 ¼ cup refrigerated pesto
   1 cup cooked chopped or shredded chicken
   3 green onions, sliced
   1 tomato, chopped
   8 ounces (2 cups) LAND O LAKES® Chedarella® Cheese, shredded

• Heat gas grill on medium or charcoal grill until coals are ash white.

• Brush 1 side of each tortilla with melted butter. Place buttered-side down onto ungreased baking sheet. Spread 1 tablespoon pesto over each tortilla. Top with chicken, green onions and tomato. Sprinkle with cheese.

• Place pizzas onto grill. Close lid; grill until cheese is melted and crust is crisp (3 to 6 minutes). Cut into wedges.

tip:
Shred the meat from a hot, ready-to-eat whole deli rotisserie chicken to make preparation easy.

Grilled Sourdough Bread with Garden Tomatoes

Preparation time: **15 minutes** | Grilling time: **6 minutes** | **4 servings**

   ¼ cup LAND O LAKES® Butter
   2 tablespoons chopped shallots or onion
   ½ teaspoon finely chopped fresh garlic
   4 (½-inch) slices round sourdough bread
   ¼ cup torn fresh basil leaves
   2 medium Roma tomatoes, each cut into 6 slices
   2 teaspoons red wine vinegar

• Heat gas grill on medium or charcoal grill until coals are ash white.

• Melt butter in 1-quart saucepan until sizzling; stir in shallots and garlic. Cook over medium heat, stirring occasionally, until shallots are tender (1 to 2 minutes).

• Place bread slices onto grill. Grill until toasted (4 to 6 minutes). Turn; brush each bread slice with butter mixture. Sprinkle with basil; top each bread slice with 3 tomato slices. Sprinkle each tomato-topped bread slice with ½ teaspoon vinegar.

• Continue grilling until bread is lightly browned (2 to 3 minutes).

Teriyaki Chicken Lettuce Wraps

Preparation time: **30 minutes** | Grilling time: **12 minutes** | **4 servings, 12 wraps**

- 4 (4-ounce) boneless skinless chicken breast halves
- ⅔ cup teriyaki marinade, reserve 1 tablespoon
- ½ cup uncooked instant long-grain rice
- ½ cup boiling water
- ½ cup chopped cucumber
- ½ cup chopped red bell pepper
- 2 green onions, sliced
- 2 tablespoons dry roasted peanuts, chopped
- 2 tablespoons chopped fresh cilantro
- 1 tablespoon mayonnaise
- 12 bib lettuce leaves

• Place chicken and teriyaki marinade, except 1 tablespoon, in large resealable plastic food bag. Tightly seal bag; place into 13×9-inch pan. Refrigerate, turning bag occasionally, at least 30 minutes.

• Heat gas grill on medium-high or charcoal grill until coals are ash white. Remove chicken from marinade; discard marinade. Place chicken onto grill. Close lid; grill, turning once, until chicken is no longer pink and juices run clear when pierced with a fork (12 to 16 minutes). Coarsely chop grilled chicken.

• Meanwhile, place rice into medium bowl. Add boiling water; stir. Cover tightly with plastic food wrap; let stand 5 minutes or until water is absorbed.

• Combine rice, remaining 1 tablespoon teriyaki marinade, chopped chicken and all remaining ingredients except lettuce in medium bowl; mix well.

• To serve, spoon about ⅓ cup chicken mixture onto each lettuce leaf; fold or roll up lettuce leaf.

Tomato & Roasted Garlic Tart

Preparation time: **25 minutes** | Baking time: **58 minutes** | **12 servings**

    1 large garlic bulb
    1 teaspoon olive oil
    1 sheet frozen puff pastry, thawed
    4 medium (2 cups) Roma tomatoes, thinly sliced
    ¼ teaspoon salt
    5 ounces (1¼ cups) LAND O LAKES® Chedarella® Cheese, finely shredded
    ½ teaspoon dried basil leaves, crushed
    ¼ teaspoon freshly ground pepper

• Heat oven to 375°F. Slice top off garlic bulb, exposing cloves. Place onto large piece of aluminum foil; drizzle with olive oil. Fold aluminum foil over garlic to seal. Place onto ungreased small baking sheet. Bake for 45 to 50 minutes or until garlic is very tender. Remove from oven; cool completely.

• Meanwhile, line another baking sheet with parchment paper. Roll out puff pastry on parchment paper-lined baking sheet into 11-inch square. Pinch pastry to form ¼-inch edge. Prick bottom with fork; cover with plastic food wrap. Refrigerate for 30 minutes.

• Lightly sprinkle tomatoes with salt; place onto paper towels to remove excess moisture. Pat dry.

• Increase oven temperature to 425°F. Squeeze roasted garlic from skins into small bowl; mash with fork. Spread over bottom of pastry. Top with ¾ cup cheese. Arrange tomatoes in rows on top of cheese; sprinkle with basil and pepper. Top with remaining cheese. Bake for 13 to 16 minutes or until pastry is golden brown and cheese is melted.

tip:
To save time in preparing this tart, bake the garlic the day before and refrigerate until ready to use.

Maple-Glazed Beef Short Ribs

Preparation time: **30 minutes** | Cooking time: **62 minutes** | Grilling time: **20 minutes** | **6 servings**

Ribs

4 pounds beef short ribs
5 cups water

Glaze

¼ cup LAND O LAKES® Butter
1 medium (½ cup) onion, chopped
1 cup pure maple or maple-flavored syrup
½ cup apple cider
¼ cup soy sauce
2 tablespoons stone-ground mustard
½ teaspoon salt

• Combine ribs and water in 5-quart saucepan or Dutch oven. Cover; cook over medium heat, stirring occasionally, until water comes to a full boil (10 to 15 minutes). Reduce heat to low; cook until ribs are tender (30 to 35 minutes). Drain; pat dry.

• Meanwhile, melt butter in 2-quart saucepan until sizzling; add onion. Cook over medium heat, stirring occasionally, until onion is softened (6 to 8 minutes). Stir in all remaining glaze ingredients. Continue cooking, stirring occasionally, until mixture comes to a full boil (6 to 8 minutes). Reduce heat to medium-low. Cook, stirring occasionally, until sauce thickens slightly and flavors blend (15 to 20 minutes). Reserve ½ cup glaze.

• Heat one side of gas grill on medium or charcoal grill until coals are ash white. Place coals to one side in charcoal grill. Make aluminum foil drip pan; place opposite coals.

• Place ribs on grill over drip pan. Cover; grill, turning occasionally and brushing with reserved ½ cup glaze, until ribs are fork tender and heated through (20 to 25 minutes). Serve with remaining hot glaze.

tip:
Leftover glaze can also be used on chicken or pork. Brush glaze on during last 10 minutes of grilling.

tip:
Ribs are precooked to shorten grilling time and to tenderize meat.